Ig'nant

Social Media's Twitter and Facebook Users Most Ignorant Tweets and Posts!

Boost Your Business Strategy & Marketing Success By Avoiding Blogging Pitfalls

Ben Popp

Nowadays it is unbelievable what the masses tweet and post publicly online. Their messages are sometimes funny, ignorant, serious and inappropriate. Which all in all make the rockin social media world go round. Oh, and also can make them unemployed. Yet there are those brave bloggers who fear not the handout seekers, pot stirrers, media firestorms and opinions of the people. For they are what this country needs now more than ever.

R.I.P. #freedomofspeech ?

#inyourdreamspilgrim

Book Lingo

\# = tweet

no # post = facebook

idc = I don't care

fml = fuck my life

nm = never mind

lol = laugh out loud

yolo= you only live once

rofl=rolling on floor laughing

much misspelled wordage, jive, and slang to accurately portray current social media.

A Humor Book

Doesn't it seem like if you are born with rosy cheeks and pale skin, you are destined to be a meat cutter at like a Sam's Club or Walmart? Right?

When you get stuck behind an elderly Jeralamima buying her lotto quik picks with all of her out of wedlock nieces and nephews birthdays etc. #lol #SuperstitiousShanaynays

Interpretation of a Puffs cereal commercial: Dear African Americans, we have provided a mulatto kid rapper to rap nearby a Puffs cereal box so this is how we plan to hook you in..

Lol when you give a bulldyke "empire carpeting's" phone number in place your girlfriend's to "hang out."
#Empirestateofmind

Got dumped by my girlfriend today when she introduced me to her Korean War Veteran grandfather. I was so intimidated the first thing I said was "how is your prostate?" #fml #Flomax

Can your migraines come from when you were in the womb and rogue sausages poked your dome? #outofaspirin

Lol when grandpa can't clear his computer history.
#sundaydinners

My football team had to run extra laps because I crossed out "Hugh Jackman" on my coach's anniversary card from his wife, and added "as sexy as the 70's fisherman in Jaws who scrapes his nails down the chalkboard" #farewellinthedunes

Lotta girls have diaper ass. Not like a huge butt, or a small butt, but like a bundled up bunch of clothes wedged in those wranglers.
#huggiessquad

Lol Disney lol.. having a handful of animated characters have deep southern ebony voices in each movie just to cover their politically correct bases.. #AngryMadeaMothers

When you see a classmate or peer of yours with a shitty half grown mustache, doesn't it seem like THEY were the ones who left turds in the ballpit at McDonald's when you were young? #sweatyarcadekids

Did my homework at the VFW last night. Mom's going to be pissed… lol #drunkdaddyprobz #thirdgrader

When your little brother ask pops for more token money at Chuckee Cheese.. #laidoff #saddad #bolognasandwhiches

Bonded out my dad last night and collected his belongings: one brown trenchcoat. #dadsapervert #fortonightsexhibition

Lol when a Mexican landscaper sees you trimming your pubes on the couch and keeps working..

Wtf.. there's only one black sitcom… idc nm, lol

Low-income-ites eggs
seem the most fertile..
#seemslike

Pass bamacare already! STFU yall some lames governmint

Have you seen Barbara Walter's 2014 top most fascinating people list yet? Yeah, #deeznuts

Homo ass.. if u wuz a
pokemon you'd b
called PUFFINS

Ggguurll you bout sexy as Don King's hearin aid

I'm not a bushman of the Kalahari ya dig? I'll settle for a landing strip #pilotlyfe #muffsquad

"Wouldn't it be nice" remix: if Latin jugs sprayed horchata, African jugs leaked chocolate milk, white jugs tapped 2%

Tired of doing my bro's laundry.. Oughta invest in Shout! #skidrow #skidmarkshark

Prairiedoggin it at Walmart checkout #yolo

taping a cucumber to my leg before hittin the club #hungsolo #veggietaleimpaler lmao at these gringos swearin they Indian. #sketcherswearinass #moccasinless everytime the news mentions "teabaggers" in politics I lose my shit guey jajaja ever notice 1980's adult film chicks are all about lickin the sides of the shaft? #thatstheshitIdontlike

I bet the long nailed retro mature lady in the perfume section of the mall right now serviced Don Johnson in the 1980's..

Who didn't get a chubby watchin the pink power ranger in the 1990's? #90'schildhood

Tryna buy my son a bike helmet. None fit.. #bigheadass #superdome

That look you get when you try to pay for your halloween costume with a hundred at the thrift store…
#puebloproblems
#sillymestizo
#Columbus
#whitemanbringfirewater

Call me crazy, but doesn't every Giordano's Pizza Restaurant busboy have the same haircut? #prohibitionerafade #johndillingerdew

Steak too well done?
Enjoy your fillet O'Taint
bitchy customer.
#awaiterslife
#dingleberrydelight

In the paper today I guess a dead whale washed up on the beach and some kids spray painted a giant dick on it lol. That's how I want to go out

Politicians who snap pics of their junk and send it to their girlfriends should be applauded. At least their straight #ugh #leadersAmericaneeds read the bulletin board my community has at its rec center, and I guess coyotes have been eating old folks purse dogs! They think its from neighbors throwing leftover food out in the fields.. But I don't want it to go to waste? Lmao

Set up a blind date for my best bro with a chick who sports Brian Bosworth's dew in his prime! #nojoke #ToBozorBuzz

Found out last night's smash had one eye.. Feelin like a straight up goonie cuz. #oneeyedwille

Why does every African American commercial mom have the Macy Gray afro and kakis?

Just got pulled over textin and drivin. Gonna tag the police department in this post lmfao

Steady crop dusting this entire movie theatre right now. Don't cut the tape, cut the cheese.

My boi dropped a Lincoln log. Clogged da toilet. N bounced out from dis party before dis gurl's pops was a'plungin. lmao fuckin goon

As a kid didn't it seem like it was called the Searuss Tower and not Sears Tower? Guess it's Sears Tower #fyi #themoreyouknow just got fired from my job today n shit for posting party pics from the weekend.. rofl look who's gonna milk Uncle Sam's tiggo bitties? #me #unemployed if I was a social media addicted burglar, I'd "check in" at the house I was robbing what do you feed your fighting hobo? That thing can fight! Dam, that fucker almost bit me.. Watch #bumsbrawl #bogusasfuck

If I had the choice between being suffocated with a pillow in the hospital or being suffocated between Dolly Parddon's blue veiny milk canteens, I'd go with option 2

In his broken English, this Philippino guy I work with on a cruise ship told me he doesn't get to see his family for nine months at a time! I shook my head in recognition of his circumstance. Turned my head away from him in the elevator. and lol

Man joe, if I had inherited a farm wif generations and generations of fam passin down the farmin tradition, I'd sell dat mo fucka. Phuckin hick ass, overall wearin, count em by the bushel ass bitches. Yo land developers let me holla at chu

At a boring ass colonial settlement tour, listening to this Quaker Oats lookin gilf give a spiel on the importance turkeys have had on our culture. I'm blindly nodding along. #GOBBLETHESENUTS

At work I just cut a hole under the Dunkin Doughnuts box so my package can sprawl out amongst the leftover crumbs under a closed lid. My buddy thinks there is one doughnut left! Keep you posted if he's gay or not

Got my mom's facebook account shutdown for one because I don't want her snooping, and two because I kept reporting her inappropriate comments I concocted on her page. Lmao she bought all these how-to social media books before hand!

Past couple days she's been cleaning her coke bottle glasses wondering what went wrong! #dying

Ya like wendy's? When Deez Nuts bounce off your chin! #sleepover #buddysasleep #ballsoneyes #shaftrestingonnose #squidwardswag #Idreamofgonzo

HATE going to the fuckin dentist.. If I could give anyone my dental care, I'd let one of those third world country infomercial kids take it in a HEARTBEAT! #ungrateful #justdontcare

Swear Doctor it was your cold hands for the physical. Not me. #shrinkage #choadsquad #rotiniweeni

My best buddy who is a children's author mind you, got wasted with me as usual last night. Ransacked our cabinet. Ate all of my twin little sisters cereals for the week. Puked outside our door stoop. Passed out on my bed while I had the tile floor. Never knowing these chain of events, my sisters wanted his autograph still.. #wtf

Picking dad up again from the bar. Dudes got like.. a file cabinet full of D.U.I.'s lol #hitandrun #thebighouse #humanshishkabob

At catholic elementary school I was ALWAYS in the principal's office for some bullshit. Harmless stuff like drawing dicks on classmates folders or drawing soul brothers with obnoxious afro's

Stanky bref. No deodorant. Skid mark tint in da draws. #itsawonderfullyfe #allguyschool #militaryacademy

No joke, honkey in the steam room is a horse..
#MrEd

Lovin these local loans commercials! Always some dug-up hoodrat with a gold tooth who either talks slick, or is unattractively uber bucksome

Grounded for flinging my dog's poop I was supposed to pick up over the neighbor's fence. I have a great dane. They have a miniature pincher lol

My second grader's daddy is sssoo smoking hot right now at conferences xoxo #DILF #sweetdickwilly #teacherproblems

Was not a fan of eating bananas at lunch throughout my school years. EVERYONE knows that guys who eat bananas like dongs. or want to believe they fancy dongs. Right?

Impossible to keep a straight face when I tell my bank I signed some form to where I am able to not pay overdrafts lmfao #rookiecocksucker #dduurr

Giirrll, any yall got a
high buttcrack like me?
fuckin shits like
climbing my back lolol

Ok, so when are corey's parents on boy meets world gonna mate in the family room in front of everyone?! JEEZ.. their always necking and grinding privates when one of their kids are spilling their guts out about some sappy age-unrealistic dilemma

Saying thank you in every language EXCEPT Chinese at this Chinese restaurant. Waiter seems annoyed lol #wecantstop #creamofsomeyoungguy #floormeat #sweetnsourpower snoring dad got pillow whipped at his dome. Woke up violently, spraining his neck. Next day, he vists the doctor. L.......O.........L

My son's kindergarten teacher left me a bitchy message on the machine. She asked what the kids watched last night, and mine said Scarface with dad. Haha bc fuck those obnoxious kid network shows. #DCFSmyass ha Mom must have found my knives under my pillows again when making my bed.. I hear lecturing from afar. #idc #itsfunny

Gandhi had some wack getup yo..
#cokebottleglasses
#togaass

puked outside with the bros. after, juked with the hoes. #lastnight #yackedandmacked #barfscarf

I just start selling shit of my own when I need money. Gotta be more careful though because my foster mother found her own crafts being sold on ebay by me

good way to get the money owed to you from a friend is to steal his mail every day after postman comes.
#latepayments
#feesplease
#waterofflightsoff

mission accomplished just in time last night at dark. Made cock helmet mushroom prints on the new, wet cement park slab.

I bet those dirty chimney sweepers in Mary Poppins were a hung bunch why does my dad and bro send me pics of their feces?? Eats my battery like crazy. Lol I need new family #lincolnlog #prairiedoggerz #bowlstainerz

That orphanage up the
street should change
the school fight name
to the fighting orphans

tryna mate tonite. Whose down?

try to ask an authentic Mayan to pronounce "world." Shits hilarious!

lol didn't know gurls could feel a chub when they're sitting on your lap. Woops.
#carpooling
#pickapantleg
#thinkofallthosetimes

is it me or does anyone else see dogs pooping every time you drive by a house

If my boss was perched on a branch right now in a tree sitting next to an owl, I wouldn't be able to tell who is who! #owllookinass #hootordie only important fact I took away from biology class: lions cock helmets are barbed fo real dough, 2Pac oughta be up dere in da history books wit pope john paul, momma tereza n all dem

You can always count on not getting carded by the polish immigrant lady workin the 24 hour gas station half liquor store counter #underagerrager #greencard #babooshkaclothes

It was seriously mammary fest downtown last night. #holaaeriola #brail #pancake #silverdollas tired of this non stop Olympics coverage. They work so hard blah blah blah. You know what works hard if not harder? My wash n dryer

learn our language.
Wretched swine.
Period. #USA

nothing like a hardened lesbian sighting

ever notice how foreigners take up the whole sidewalk?? They pretend they don't know USA public etiquette

As a grateful nation,
the masses oughta
rimjob veterans and
perform the rustiest of
trombones

had this Ukrainian bartender for my bachelor party, and she totally could have been Dracula's bride or was an extra in Van Helsing

my partner and I jus
got to the crime scene.
Fuckin gross lol

it should be the "Jizzard" of OZ and not WIZZARD.. #innocencetarnish #originalsucked #tinmanlionscarecrowa rebitchmade went to the bread line for shits n gigs with my bros. #freefood #middleclass #lol

can you buy libido free puppies??
#snippedsquad
#multiplenipples

had a fieldtrip with 4th grade class to a nature center.. they had an owl named Hooter! #bustyfeathers #hornballowl #milkshakebringsallth ecreaturestothebranch if I had a nickel for all of the mullets I seen at antique shows this year, I'd be on Forbes

Southern analogies suck BIG O'L F'NORGUS. Like "healthy as a.." How bout ya accept the union kicked your dicks inward?

if you could live in any jugs time period what would you choose? Saloon jugs? Colonial jugs? Conquistador Jugs? Or Medieval Jugs? #decisionsdecisions #ignoranceisbliss the best tasting foods are shaped like dicks. I came up with that. #superbad #royaltiesnow

Any cruiseship musician can attest to the dumbass questions, inquiries and most of all: dumbass requests from the band for their "wedding song."
#nauticalventing
#prostateblunders
#sachelasstourists

lol when every middle aged babyboomer author on twitter says they are "social media experts." YOU DON'T GET IT! DON'T START CONVERSATIONS IN PICTURE COMMENT BOXES! #GOBACKTOWOODSTOCK

haha "don't text and drive" commercial campaigns

fictional cartoon parents ought to run a background check on #thecatinthehat before letting their kids go with him on adventures.. #priors #catburgular #tocatchapredator

Spotting an eastern European in a lake town is easier than finding Waldo

Authors writing quarters DO smell like urine

every fast food drive
thru window girl has
crayola stenciled on
eyebrows guey

eating at a breakfast joint there is always a 99% chance that some old lady in the room is named "Ethel, Gladis, Hazel or Florence."

I wouldn't mind being some type of model for a living.. Can't be a hand one though because mine's deformed haha lol me-here's my report card. Mom-good job honey! Proud of you. Me-worked hard. Mom-here's $100! Me-I upgrade my photoshop software lmao

Almost asked the Dunkin Doughnuts manager if he was a survivor of the "Temple Of Doom." Almost..

hispanics put "CH's" in front of their "SH's." like chee was or more sheese please. Right?!

if your white and morbidly obese, chances are you could get a diabetes commercial gig. #hustlehard

"If you call on your neighbor to the alderman often!"-Next Dr.Seuss Book #longgrass #wateringpastcityhours #minorityfriendvisits hiding behind the credenza as the elderly neighbor rings the doorbell for help carrying heavy heirlooms to the attic. #fuckthatshit #payup #nothome the doctors face when you ask him if there is a way to increase your girth. Aka the width of your shaft #priceless when you ditch a recently deceased relatives funeral remembrance card, to keep room only for the escort card you got handed to you against your will in Vegas

Paused doing homework to watch that youtube video of those turtles screwing lmfao

grandma's such a royal cunt to restaurant staff.. can't imagine how many pube and dandruff burgers shes downed..
#watchwaiting

my grandfather's such a sweet old guy. Sitting behind him calling him a cheap old cocksucker in his deaf ear cracks me up how are YOU gay if your friends were the ones who insisted on teabagging you last night when you were getting REM sleep?

ever notice if you work
maintenance, that most
guys piss everywhere
BUT the bowl?

what do they do with the unwanted mamories after breast reduction surgeries? #curiouslikegeorge don't care if the neighbors see me nude. Hate fuckin with the blinds

The "Merry Christmas ya filthy animal" guy in Home Alone seems like in real life he would be a horseshit grandpa

I had to wait in line at the E R because minorities had papercuts.. #ihadkidneystones #wtf on the tv service provider commercials, why are families all smiling so much and like at the same time?

getting demoted at work now lol. Lecture's boring as a mofo. Gunna check my twitter feed lmfao when you create a fake facebook account of a hot chick and add your dad as a friend! Watch how fast he accepts and messages her #dumbdilf #momsmuffintop cant believe this friend of ours STILL hangs out with us after an entire childhood or calling his mom a whore, stripper who serviced strangers just so my buddy could have steady lunchables. What assholes we were

Asked this retro mature lady to sleep with me at my buddy's lakehouse. She said no. So I asked her "what were the 70's like?"

Hey uum, so does anybody have like a friend or know a friend who can do a rhinoplasty quick garage surgery or something?? Looking for a discounted quick nasal straightening. #rhinonose #pinnochioschnozz #donttellinsurance

I bet Robin Williams was the biggest adhd kid in elementary school history. My heart goes out to all of his past teachers..

Many future guests on the show COPS think Axe bodyspray is a fair substitute for a shower. #gymclass

Gotta feed the parrots material.. Friends that copy your humor and are tragically born without the ability to generate their own material? Here's a 8" cracker for you parrots #pollywantasausage

Why does every mother who has offspring victim to gun violence, only possess a third grade graduation photo of their kid?

Can you call the Orkin man when you live in a pineapple under the sea, infested with ants?

rappel down my gooch rope

take your misbehaved kids out of the movie theatre hoodrat parents with multiple children out of wedlock. It's a midnight showing.. uh, its fucking bedtime for kids everywhere?

When the neighbor kids put flaming bags of poop on my doorstep, I feel like the Scooby Doo villain when he says "you meddling kids.."

lol if "Ernest" the movie character was told to "take a seat" by the To Catch A Predator Host!

turned big 21 today!! Stoppin for Friday class at Sylvan Learning Center then hittin the town! #barcrawl #classsucks

Started naming the bums we see daily at work. Trying to figure out which is my favorite.. #hm #ministrysquad lol would be funny if gilfs scooted when they were in heat! #catscratchfever the countryass foreman of mine at this construction site looks straight up like the Count from Seaseme Street. I aint shittin ya

wonder if my boss
tried out for Pirates of
The Carribean..
#afakelegislikeakeg
#prostheticprofessional

seriously section 8 bunch sitting on the corner where I drive by you everyday.. wtf could you be possibly debating with one another?

got grounded bc mom overheard me talking about my uncle screwing this pregnant girl saying "he's on his adding genes grind" haha if you don't like a cat in your workplace, write an anonymous note to the owner from the boss relaying the message that the feline can no longer be in the work environment due to allergies and other sickness.. fuckin works great "you got more moose on your head than Yellowstone!" buddys dad is such a deufice assmunch

people with bluetooth's in public.. they should be euthanized

holy fck'n shit our new cleaning crew isn't polish!

if only my buddy knew his fiancé was my desktop background

I'm a walking libido right now

any surrounding neighbors of curious george's handler concerned that he hasn't gotten george his shots?

what happens when a mime mates with a stray mime?

asked my bro if he hooked up with these two sisters we know. He said he had with the entire litter lmfao #meowmixchicks what are the odds my brother's warrant was served on mother's day right when we sat down for supper?! #momsfacerightnow #priceless

not a fan of orangutan
jugs.. #bananas
#elfshoejugs

irritated by all these Native Americans commercials where a tear is rolling down their face. Wtf you got like a BUNCH of casinos? #heyhowareya #makingreservations notice most male cartoon characters have no package? Not even a bulge can any celebrity singer be normal? Dress normal? Wear jeans and a button up shit. Enough with this mysterious/fucked up wardrobe when I die: schedule the wake. dress me in dirty sweats. Throw me in a dilapidated box. Give everyone the wrong address so no one comes to my wake. So the the only guy there is the maintenance guy who has to look at me all day in pitty!

was not a fan of overweight elementary teachers who would put their fupa(big bladder popping from jeans) in your face when you needed help with your homework..

Coffeeshop dwellers. Finish your latte and conform to mainstream society. Be blue collar and grumble about work. Not a hipster who will oppose the general consensus on most topics.

how funny would that be if spongebob got two years in a Turkish prison for not having his passport?

british people have bad teeth. #crest #floss #brush

so do Romanians still have the only occupation of traveling gyspy in a horse carriage? Like the ones with all of their tacky, superstitious junk clanking around?

had multiple tv's I couldn't sell at my appliance store delivered and setup to an Amish village lol

I was supposed to watch my grandparents house for a month while they traveled outside the country. Instead I said the hell with it, and rented it out to some mangy white bikers. Hopefully they took grandma's hideous jewelry. #eyesore rippin ass in this line at the DMV. Wish it was more pungent than the overwhelming smell of corn tortillas and stale du-rag..

my family's in love with the new st Bernard next door. Best thing I love bout him is his loafs he's gonna pinch that make perfect flaming bags of shit for bitch neighbors.

it's always the cockblock at parties that puts on those messed up viral videos for everyone to gather around to see

I wish we lived in a society where people fulfilled their stereotypes..

Just bought Pee Wee's Playhouse. "Chairy's" face is priceless after designating that his chair will be the main beatoff station. #browneyebandit #stainsmgee #pinkeye

immediately returning
my first communion
gifts.
#newgrandtheftauto
#instores

who else had to "go back to the car" because they picked up the penis looking gourds at pumpkin patches and made gestures with them?

would you rather be on a rotisserie over a witch's caldron? Or do 20 years in prison for being framed for breaking into a sperm bank to steal samples?

politically correct commercials… lol what a crock

**illiterate adults make
me sick to my stomach**

that'd be sweet if we
had kangaroo pouches
to carry shit around in
ya know

this guy. My friend's been pumping up his Halloween costume for months now. Its obvious his mom spent more on her Paul Malls than her son's favorite holiday #walgreenshalloween mask

honkey mo fuckas
don't like Sanford n
Son. bet

fiancé's dad kicked me out of the big dinner.. made sure I ate and drank first before I broke the news about the mandatory pre-nup I require
#worrywart #square

made an app that requires college students to log-on in the same location when taking tests; to prevent paid friends from taking them. Gonna piss a whole lot of people off. #lifeshardthenyoudie seriously, any highschooler should party at a Mexican bar. They don't card for SHIT! Wish I would have known that in highschool.

people from Luxemburg eat their dinner with desserts? I could MAYBE see Chex Mix sweet and salty bags but. #turnamerican #whatareyouwaitingfor if you're ever looking to hire a busboy, seek out the shitty, suped up beaters on the road. You know, the ones with tinted windows and tacky rims? 100% chance of a busboy in there hate having swamp ass after a hot summer day in classes. Ready to ditch these briefs any second. There's not enough bleach in the world to get this hashbrownie out my best friend wants to move to a big city. He likes skyscrapers, lattes, peacoats n all that shit. Someone slap that pale shitbum my school ought to have not a food drive, but a Lubiderm drive. Ashy elbows are rampant down yonder im just disgusted. Im just disgusted when I just heard that record labels make busty singers press down their breasts bc their target market consists of youth. Why did we fight wars in the first place then?

do illegal aliens do job apps for people?? They into that sort of thing? Or are they even picky nowadays?..

if I see one more of these cocksuckin ants on my countertop..

to see a male cry during a movie.. the one word that comes to mind "broke-back mountain"

I bet our sturdy Russian waitress still has teen heartthrob posters of Putin somewhere laying around..

Lost 80lbs! what does the family do to celebrate? Book a party at Golden Corall. #fml #noonecares

was flipping through old family photos and compared my old nanny's face next to our jug of syrup. The Aunt Jamima resemblance is uncanny!